CHARLES IVES

WASHINGTON'S BIRTHDAY

First Movement of
A Symphony: New England Holidays

This edition has the approval of the Charles Ives Society, Inc., which is furthering and supporting the preparation of critical editions, both new and revised, of the music of Charles Ives. The work of the Society has been made possible by grants from the American Academy and Institute of Arts and Letters, and by a generous bequest from the late Wladimir and Rhoda Lakond.

AMP 8024

ASSOCIATED MUSIC PUBLISHERS, Inc.

Distributed by
 Hal Leonard Publishing Corporation
7777 West Bluemound Road P.O. Box 13819 Milwaukee, WI 53213

ISBN 0-7935-0431-7

PREFACE

In the *Memos* of 1932 (Norton 1972), Ives dictated: "A set of pieces for orchestra called *Holidays* had its career from 1897 to 1913. ...[S]ome organ pieces for a Thanksgiving Service [1897]... were put into a single piece for an orchestra... around 1904. I remember taking it to copy out when I went to Saranac Lake the following summer in 1905. However, this made me think of making a kind of Holiday Symphony, each movement based on something of the memory a man has of his boy holidays."

But it was four years later (on Columbus Day) that he started another one, whose score-sketch (1912?) is headed: "New England Holidays—I. 'Washington's Birthday'—started Oct. 22, 1909, at 70 W. 11." The full score (1913?) is entitled: "Washington's Birthday (in the 70's)"—a decade he would have known more by later hearsay than by his own memory.

Apparently the *Holidays* underwent some uncertainty of medium. On a sketch of *Emerson*, Ives wrote: "Piano Sonata #3, N.E. Holidays." But the first version of *Decoration Day* (complete in ink) is for violin and piano, headed: "Sonata #5, N.E. Holidays"—and sketches of *Washington's Birthday* seem to betray a violin-and-piano origin. Ives was often reticent about how his music evolved, and nowhere else is there any hint that the *Holidays* were ever non-orchestral.

The *Memos* go on to say: "The *Washington's Birthday* is for a kind of chamber orchestra: strings, 1 horn, 1 flute, a set of bells, and in the chorus a Jew's harp ad lib. I've always been a good Jew's harp player regardless of consequences, but I don't know exactly how to write for it. The notes on the Jew's harp are but some of the partials of a string, and its ability to play a diatonic tune is more apparent than real. And in this piece, from a half a dozen to a hundred Jew's harps are neccessary—one would hardly be heard. In the old barn dances, about all the men would carry Jew's harps in their vest pockets or in the calf of their boots, and several would stand around on the side of the floor and play the harp more as a drum than as an instrument of tones.

"The first part of this piece is but to give the picture of the dismal, bleak, cold weather of a February night near New Fairfield (for full description see program at back of music). The middle part and the shorter last part are but kinds of refrains made up of some of the old barn-dance tunes and songs of the day (half humorous, half sentimental, and half serious). As I remember some of these dances as a boy, and also from Father's description of some of the old dancing and fiddle playing, there was more variety of tempo than in the present-day dances. In some parts of the hall a group would be dancing a polka, while in another a waltz, with perhaps a quadrille or lancers going on in the middle." [Compare the three-orchestra scene in *Don Giovanni* and the three deck-orchestras in Ives's *The General Slocum*.]

"Some of the players in the band would, in an impromptu way, pick up with the polka, and some with the waltz or march. Often the piccolo or cornet would throw in 'asides.' Sometimes the change in tempo and mixed rhythms would be caused by a fiddler who, after playing three or four hours steadily, was getting a little sleepy—or by another player who had been seated too near the hard cider barrel.

"Whatever the reason for these changing and sometimes simultaneous playings of different things, I remember distinctly catching a kind of music that was natural and interesting, and which was decidedly missed when everybody came down 'blimp' on the same beat again. The allegro part of this *Washington's Birthday* aims to reflect this, as well as to depict some of the old breakdown tunes and backwoods fun and comedy and conviviality that are gradually being forgotten.

This was completed and scored out in the summer of 1913, though some of the barn-dance stuff had been used before....

"These holiday movements are but attempts to make pictures in music of common events in the lives of common people (that is, of fine people), mostly of the rural communities."

As the postface quotes Whittier's *Snow-bound*, the opening music probably quotes some no longer familiar song of wintry association, but the only fragments so far recognized are possibly the upbeat of *Home, Sweet Home* and the first measure of *Old Folks at Home*. From (J) into (K) the music seems "to go forth and see the snow on the trees"—with snatches of *Turkey in the Straw* and the *Sailor's Hornpipe* as if already heard from the barn.

The barn dance may be entirely old tunes. Those so far identified include: (in N) *Sailor's Hornpipe* (or *College Hornpipe*), *The Camptown Races*, (O) *Marlbrough s'en va t'en guerre (For He's a Jolly Good Fellow)*, (P) *The White Cockade, Turkey in the Straw (Zip Coon), Massa's in de Cold Ground*, (R) *The Campbells Are Coming, Garryowen*, (S) *Fisher's Hornpipe, Saint Patrick's Day*—many of the entrances being off-beat against the on-beat tunes, as noted in the postface.

The Andante that follows may also be derived from now forgotten songs, with a lone fiddler murmuring the *Pig Town Fling* (or *Warm Stuff*) and *Turkey in the Straw*, until a distant echo of *Good Night, Ladies* fades into the numb cold.

In *Memos* Ives also recounts a fairly satisfactory run-through with theater musicians in 1913 or '14, a frustrating attempt with symphony men in 1918 or '19, and Slonimsky's fluent performance in 1931.

JOHN KIRKPATRICK
1974

EDITOR'S NOTE

The task of editing *Washington's Birthday* is considerably hampered by the incomplete primary source. Ives's full score (1913?), herein identified as "**M**," is now missing a third of its pages (losing mm. 58-165); moreover, one third of the extant pages lack either their upper or lower halves.

This state of affairs leaves to an editor only the possibility generally of a careful combing through the copyist's full score (**T**) in search of possible omissions, confusions, mechanical errors, and inconsistencies. Beyond this, one has to take into account the evidence in m. 180 that Ives made some significant changes in 1937 on a now lost set of proof pages for the New Music publication of the score.

This editing of *Washington's Birthday*, therefore, can be said to have been carefully and respectfully but, at times, only intuitively handled. Given the paucity of complete sources, the Critical Commentary is shorter than it might have been, but it should be consulted thoroughly for performance or research purposes.

JAMES B. SINCLAIR
New Haven, Connecticut, January 1987

This edition is based on materials in the Charles Ives Collection, John Herrick Jackson Music Library, Yale University, New Haven, Connecticut.

INSTRUMENTATION

Flute (doubling Piccolo)

Horn in F

Bells

Jew's Harp(s)

Strings

EDITORIAL COMMENT

The string writing assumes no more than 88664; best performed with 66442.

Ives writes that the Bells [orchestra bells] are to be "played lightly throughout or at a distance. If no bells, a piano may play the part."

The Jew's Harp(s) are indicated to "sound" in A -A -F; Ives says that "this part may be taken by 2 Clarinets, omitting the middle note (where there are 3)."

Additionally, "if the string orchestra is large, a Trombone or Bassoon may reinforce the 1st Cello part from (P) to (W)."

Conductors should also read these entries in the Critical Commentary following the music: 9-11 Vn2 and Va, 19-21 Fl and Vn2, 32 B1, 65 Vc, 67 Vc, 70 Fl, 149 Vn2/b.

duration: ca. 9 minutes

Performance material is available from the publisher on rental.

WASHINGTON'S BIRTHDAY

CHARLES IVES

Edited by James B. Sinclair

6

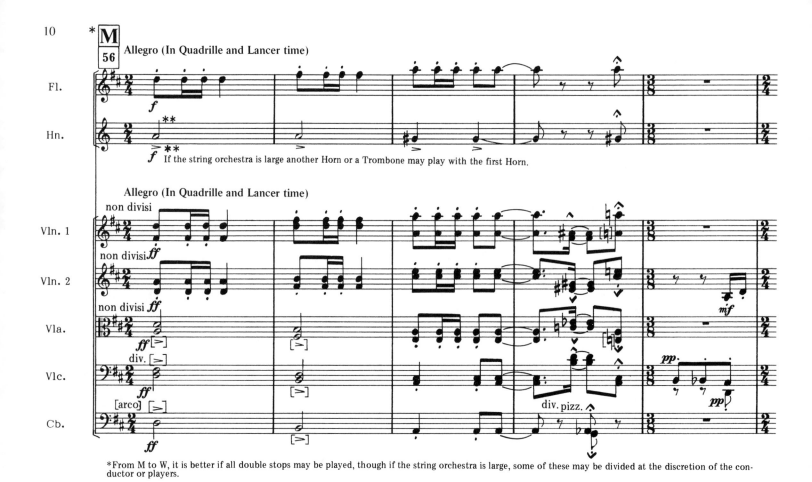

*From M to W, it is better if all double stops may be played, though if the string orchestra is large, some of these may be divided at the discretion of the conductor or players.

12

14

*Let Horn play this in place of Flute,

if the string orchestra is large (not both).

*This part may be taken by 2 Clarinets, omitting the middle note where there are 3.

† As indicated, it is important to note, in pages **15-22** where the "off beats" in various parts bear the heavy accent and where not.

✶✶If the string orchestra is large, a Trombone or Bassoon may reinforce the first Cello part from P. to W.

*Only a few 2nd Violins play this, the others playing with the 1st Violins.

18

** It will be noticed that the Viola part from here through (S) contains the harmony going with both keys—that of the 1st Violin and Horn. If played divisi, use fewer players with Horn chords. (See Viola, lines between).

*1/2 arco / 1/2 pizz.

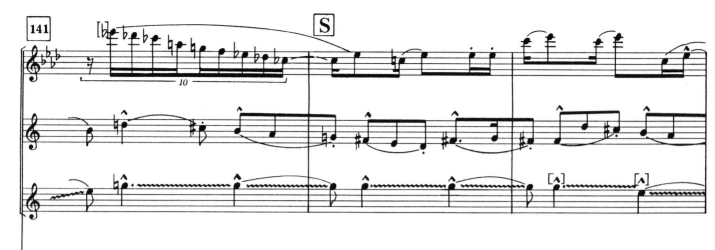

*If there are but few 1st Violins, all 2nd Violins may play throughout at Director's discretion.

28

*Unless the string orchestra is large, the lower Bell part may be omitted; but the violin playing the "pizz." continues. The upper Bell part may be used with a small number of strings, if played lightly enough or at a distance, or both parts for Bells may be played on piano.

*Unless string orchestra is large, or the flute may be off stage, a violin may play these strains.

POSTFACE

Ives appended the following text (in typescript) to the full score copied out by Emil Hanke. In it he quotes from John Greenleaf Whittier's poem "Snow-bound." Ives's text is given here with only the lightest editing of orthographic details and clarification of punctuation.

—J.B.S

"Cold and solitude," says Thoreau, "are friends of mine. Now is the time before the wind rises to go forth and see the snow on the trees."

And there is at times a bleakness, without stir but penetrating, in a New England midwinter, which settles down grimly when the day closes over the broken hills. In such a scene it is as though nature would but could not easily trace a certain beauty in the sombre landscape!—in the quiet but restless monotony! Would nature reflect the sternness of the Puritan's fibre or the self-sacrificing part of his ideals?

The older folks sit

"…the clean winged hearth about,
Shut in from all the world without,
Content to let the north wind roar
In baffled rage at pane and door."

—WHITTIER

But to the younger generation, a winter holiday means action!—and down through "Swamp Hollow" and over the hill road they go, afoot or in sleighs, through the drifting snow, to the barn dance at the Centre. The village band of fiddles, fife and horn keeps up an unending "breakdown" medley, and the young folks "salute their partners and balance corners" till midnight. As the party breaks up, the sentimental songs of those days are sung, and with the inevitable "adieu to the ladies" the "social" gives way to the grey bleakness of the February night.

DESCRIPTION OF SOURCES

In the descriptions, photo reproduction numbers follow the citation of each page—first, the negative photostat number(s), preceded by their appropriate letter, and second, the microfilm frame number, preceded by the letter "f."

s[1] = Pencil sketch (n1566&3172/f0711), m. 22-44 etc.; above 32-33: "also end".

s[2] = Pencil sketch, in 3-stave systems, with some orchestrational notations; upper Rh corner: "C E Ives 70 W11 [NYC] 445 Chelsea [phone]."
> one page (n0789/f0660), m. 43-55 title: "Holiday Snow storm   Washington's Birthday in New Engl[and]."

S = Ink score-sketch, on 4-stave systems, with copious pencil revision (1916 for **R**?) and orchestrational notations.
> p.1 (n0785/f0661), m. 1-18 title: "[New E]ngland Holidays   I. 'Washington's Birthday' started Feb 22—1909 at 70 W.11" [address good 25 June 1908—2 May 1911]
> p.2 (n0786/f0662) m. 19-32
> p.[3] (n0787/f0663), m. 33-49   top, bottom & Lh margins trimmed
> p.[4] (n0788/f0664), m. 50-68   top, bottom & Rh margins trimmed
> p.[5 etc.] missing, m. [69-185]

M = Full score (1913?); Ives refers to this as "old score"; oblong, with side and bottom margins trimmed on title page and p. 1-3; copious revisions and memos to copyist Hanke for the preparation of a set of parts [**V**?]; viola is written in alto clef (an exception to Ives's practice in scores of this type).

title page (n0791/f0665), middle: "IV (symphony) [crossed out] or Set for Orch. #2) ("Washington's Birthday")," added later "This was written before the 4th Sym was finished [1916] but after it was started [1910]," and "#1 Washington's Birthday (in the 70's)"; lower: "make 1 copy for each a & b [string lines] of each on separate staffs (same copy) & 1 flute, 1 horn in F but no basso"; below: "return Chas. E. Eves Hartsdale [NY] East 22 St NY NY [all crossed out] to me 37 Liberty St 3[662] John; above: "10 x (try enlarging by photo—same copy—) cut down to 10 x 13 for photostat."
> p.1 (n0792/f0666), m. 1-15
> p.2 (n0793/f0667&0668), m. 16-27   patch (once pinned) now hinged to m. 16 (seen in f0668)
> p.3 (n0794/f0669), m. 28-41   patch hinged to m.41
> p.4 (n0795/f0670&0671), m. 42-48   lower halfpage torn away losing m. 49-51; patch hinged to m. 46 (seen in f0671); above: "come for please & send back Monday at 37 Liberty not at house"
> p.5 (n0796/f0672&0673), m. 52-57 lower halfpage torn away losing m. 58-[66?]; patch hinged to m. 52b-55 (seen in f0673)
> p.[6-9] missing
> p.[10] (n0801/f0674), m. 166-171 upper 2/3 page and Lh margin cut away losing m. [160]-165; lower Rh: "C. E. Ives   37 Liberty St N[Y] 3663 John"; ExVn sketched in pencil in m. 166-167&171

p.[11] (n0802/f0675), m. 180-185   upper 2/3 page and Rh margin cut away losing m. 172-179.

R = Revised score pages for use by Hanke in preparing **T**, in ink (ca. early 1916?).
    p.[8?] (n0799/f0676), m. 116-132   top margin and line trimmed away losing flute staff, with memo: "for flute seen old score attached"; below: "see old score in safe 38 N[assau]" and "copy to X [m. 130] & return C E Ives 144 E.40." [good 6 Dec 1915—29 Apr 1916]; m. 126 is marked in copyist's hand "Page 11" (m. 126 begins p.12 of **T**)
    p.11 (n0798/f0677), m. 160-165

T = Full ink score, copied by Emil Hanke, with careful corrections & addenda by Ives; title (at bottom of p. 18): 'Washington's Birthday' Movement fr[om] an Orchestral Set——'Holidays' Chas. E Ives.   46 Cedar St., N.Y.C, N.Y." [good 1 May 1923—30 Apr 1926].
    p.1-18 (Q4149-65/f0678-94), m. 1-185
    p.19 (Q4166/f0695), typed postface (quotes from Whittier's "Snow-bound," lines 156, 155, 157 and 158, in that order); title: "Washington's Birthday (A movement in a set of pieces for orchestra—, 'Holidays in New England.')"

V = Set of parts, copied by Emil Hanke, few pages surviving; parts copied after Ives proofread **T**; probably used by Slonimsky for September 3, 1931 San Francisco performance.
    Violins I and II
    p.[4] (—/f0696), m. 126-132, 157-162, 175-185   Ives added some accents (∧)
    p.5 (—/f0697), m. 133-156
    p.6 (—/f0698), m. 163-174
    Viola
    p.3 (—/f0699), m. 147-185
    Cello-Bass
    p.4 (—/f0700), m. 126-152   minor corrections added by Ives
    p.5 (—/f0701), m. 153-162   minor corrections added by Ives
    p.6 (—/f0702), m. 163-185

CRITICAL COMMENTARY
Abbreviations:

Pic = piccolo	Db = bass
Fl = flute	Str = Strings
Hn = horn	Comp = compostition
Bl = bells	Orch = orchestration
Vn1 = 1st violins	Dyn = dynamic mark
Vn2 = 2nd violins	2. ♪ = 2nd sixteenth-note or value (etc.)
Vns = violins	3. ♪ = 3rd eighth-note or value (etc.)
Va = viola	4.b = fourth beat (etc.)
Vc = cello	Reh = rehearsal letter

Pitches are indicated with an underline: $\underline{CC}$ (the lowest C on the piano), $\underline{C}$, $\underline{c}$, $\underline{c}^1$, ("middle" C), $\underline{c}^2$, $\underline{c}^3$, $\underline{c}^4$, $\underline{c}^5$ (the highest pitch on the piano); all pitches are referred to at concert (sounding) pitch.

Chord pitches are grouped by the "+" sign, spelled from the bottom up. For linear strands, pitches are connected by a dash.

1 Memo: The New Music Edition score has "Note: Until M (page 8 [p.10 here]) all notes are natural unless otherwise marked except the same note or notes, directly following in the same measure. From A to M, the string parts are played 'divisi.' In the unison passages, all the strings in that part play unless a rest occurs in the same measure."

1 Vn1: The middle line was added to **T** after the copying was completed.

4 Vn1/b, 2-3.b: **M** has straight triplet ♩s; **S** has nothing; **T** as here.

7 Hn, last ♪ -m. 9: **M** has this in Vn1 (dyn: **mp**) with memo "use horn not violin."

8 Vn2 and Va: **MT** have dots above each ♯ cluster articulation, changed here to dashes *per* Ives's indication in 9-11 memo (see below) that ♯ cluster is to be "always held."

9 Va, last ♩: **M** has f̲♯ (error, meaning g̲♯]+a̲♯); **T** has g̲♯ restored by retains spurious f̲♯; **S** as here.

9-11 Vn2 and Va: **M** has memo: "In these 4 [actually 3] meas. IIVs and Viola play the secondary chord (A♮B♮C♮D♮) short, the first chord (G♯A♯C♯D♯) is always held"—presumably Ives means the first chord is held *ten.,* not held through.

12 Va and Vc/a, 2-3.♪: Ties appear in **M** only.

12 Vc, 2-3.b: **M** has  changed to "better copy" (as used here);

T has an inexplicable hybrid:

16 Vn1a/lower, 3.b: **SM** have g̲♮¹; **T** agreed but was changed to a̲♮¹ (as here).

19-21 Fl and Vn2: These quintuplets were worked out on **S** for inclusion in **M** after completion of the scoring. In the interest of coordinating these 5s in performance, an editorial option is given here for shifting the barlines. (Some of the durational values in Vn1 and Vc have been subsectioned to allow for clarification of the beat in either metering.)

20 Vn1 and Va, last ♪: **T** lacks dyn **pp**; **M** has both.

32 Bl: Ives created this part after the completion of **M**, going back to **S** to sketch the plan for a floating, barely audible glint of sound. Rhythmically the writing is disembodied from the strings, and it is nearly impossible to perform exactly as notated—and would be pointless to do so. The performance part is fully cued to the violin line. A "sync-up" cue from the conductor at Reh "K" (m. 52) should assure coordination of the important closing at 54-55.

32-33 Hn: **T** slurs 2-3. ♩ of each triplet; **M** appears to have slur under all three ♩s (better).

34 Vn1/a, 4.♪: **MT** have no accidental (implying 1.♪ ♯ carries through) but **S** has no 1.♪ <u>d</u>♯³ (added on **M**) thus 4. ♪ is <u>d</u>♮² (surely Ives's intention for here).

34 Db, 1-2.b: Only **S** has slur (used here).

35 Hn, 2.b: **S** has accent (used here).

36-38 Fl and Str, 5.b: This repeating interruption first appears as an insert for **M** (used here) worked out on **S**. **T** departs (in error?) in details from the extant materials. Perhaps Ives rewrote the insert. If **T** is correct, here is its exact articulation:

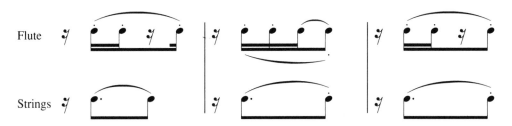

SM are clear that Str do not rearticulate the dot but cut short; **T** is confused on this.

38 Vn1/a, 3.♪; **T** has <u>f</u>♯² (error); **SM** as here.

38 Vn2/b, 6.♪: **MT** have <u>c</u>♯¹, changed on **T** to <u>d</u>♯¹ (as here); **S** has <u>d</u>♮¹.

40 Vn2/a, 5.b: **T** has <u>a</u>♯¹ (error), a misreading of **M** ♮ sign.

41,5.b-42,2.b Bl: **M** doubly enters the 3. ♩ (once at the end of its p. 3 and again at the beginning of p. 4, carried out in **T** as 4 ♩ s (corrected here).

42 Vn2/a, 2.b: **MT** have ♩ (error).

43 Tempo: **M** has "*a tempo*" (used here) missing in **T**.

43 Vn1/b, 4.b: **T** has <u>b</u>♭ (the <u>d</u>¹+<u>a</u>¹ is in Vn1/a); this misrepresents the rising line which was added on **M** (<u>b</u>♭ and <u>a</u>¹ exchanged here).

44 Vn2/a, 3.b: **s**² has ♭ (on g1) not used in **SMT** (nor here).

44 Vn1/b, 4.b: **T** lacks ♮ (added here); **s**² **S** show <u>f</u>¹ is ♮; **M** has added line (as seen here in 1-2.b) which gives ♯ for 3.♪ not intended to carry through.

50 Tempo: **S** has "quite fast" over 7-8.b (used here).

50 Db: Ives entered dyn *ff* on **T** when rightly *fff* (as here) is called for by the graduations.

52 Vc/a, 6.b: **T** has <u>f</u>♯ tied over, not in **M** (unnecessary, already in Va/a & b).

54 Comp: **SM** are heavily marked for repeat of this meas.; marked "use" on **M**, then repeats crossed out.

54 Hn: **M** has this, with memo "for horn orig. scheth" (all crossed out):

ST as here.

56 Tempo: **S** has "fast (Quadrille or Lancer time);" **M** has "(Allegro) (moderato [crossed out]) (In "Quadrille or Lancer" time)."

56 Str: **SM** dyn is *f*; Ives entered *ff* on **T** which lacked any dyn.

56-58 Hn: **S** has accents (used here) lacking in **MT**.

58-60 Comp: **S** (perhaps **M**?) has simpler ♩ ♫♩ ♩♩ | ♩̂ ⁷ ♫ | ; the change toward

the present version was sketched onto **S** (presumably for **R**).

65 Vc: **T** has the *arco/pizz. div.* start here, an unlikely change of pattern for Ives (possibly better to begin at m. 61,2.b).

67 Vc: **T** notation is exactly as here, being unclear as to whether *arco/pizz.* continues; perhaps best continued through m. 68, then all *arco* from m.69 on.

68 Vn2: **S** has 1-2.b slur.

70 Fl; In **T** this appears in m. 69; the editor assumes that this is a copyist error and that it belongs in 70 (as a parallel to treatment in 72).

114-115 Hn: Ives apparently wanted these Vc/a cues to appear here (and in 118-119, 123-126). No memo about this survives in **T**, but a memo in **R** would probably have been similar to that for m. 111: "horn may reinforce the first cello part here if the string orchestra is large (but not needed if trombone or bassoon is already helping)."

116 Vn2, 2.b: **RT** have <u>a</u>♭ +<u>d</u>♭ ¹; on **T** Ives crossed out the <u>a</u>♭ (which would double Va).

120-121 Hn: **RT** have both small face notes and measure rests here, but **T** ignores Ives's **R** memo asking for "(large notes)" (as used here).

125 Vn2, 3.♪: **R** has dyn *f*, changed on **T** to *ff* (as here).

128-129 Vn2: Only **V** has the continuing accents (added by Ives).

131 Vn1, 2.b: **RT** have ⌢ ; Ives added triplet mark "3" on **T** (note values corrected here); **V** has ⌢

141 Pic, 2.♪ : **T** has e̲ ♮ ^{3} (error?); e̲ ♭ ^{3} (as here) fits the pattern of decending clusters.

143 Va, 2.b: **T** has ♮ on a̲^{1} (surely intended for g̲^{1} as here).

149 Vn2/b, 2.♪ : The ♮ for e̲^{2} is suspect but we lack **s^{2}SM** to prove an error.

152 Vc/a, 2.b: **TV** lack last pitch (f̲ ♭) in the *gliss.* (added here in the performance part).

152 Vc/a, 2.b: **TV** lack grace note (d̲ ♮) expected by the pattern (added here).

153-156 Vn1/a: On **V** Ives added accents under each a̲^{1} + c^3 diad; **T** has accent over only first note of each quadruplet.

153-156 Vn1/b: On **V** Ives added accents under each d̲^{1} +e̲ ♭ ^{2} diad; **T** has accent over only first note of each sextuplet.

156,7.♪-157,1.♪, Jew's Harp: **T** has 3 ♪s here (under the Pic's 4 ♪s), adjusted here to effectively 2 ♪s.

161 Pic, 2.b: **R** has flat (as here) missing in **T**.

170 Vc: **M** has tie (as here) missing in **T**.

174 Hn,Vn1/a & Vn2: On **T** Ives added a *cresc.* wedge under the eighth-rest for Hn, probably intended to effect the next on-going phrase (as moved here, and also good for Vns).

175 Bl/lower, 5.♩: **T** has a̲♭ (error by Ives or Hanke?) which violates the simple pattern of alternation, changed here to b̲ ♭ .

180 Fl&Vn1/b: **T** has Fl playing top Vn line with no harmony line, Vn1 taking over from Fl on last ♩; apparently Ives altered this (as here) for the 1937 printed score (perhaps on a set of proof sheets); **M** has top line in Vn1 but crossed out, with a line trailing up (toward flute?).

181 Vn1/a: This was added later on **M** and labelled "shadow."

182 Vn1/b, last♪: From here on, **M** has rests for half section.